YOUR BUSINESS YOUR WAY

A Unique Perspective on

Business Development

Bernie Davies

"Own it, Bottle It, Sell it!"

DEDICATION

The sentiments in this book would never have rung as true as they do without my mother, Dr. Mertel Elizabeth Thompson. She taught me the value of hard work and dogged determination amidst any challenge of humble beginnings. Through serious debilitating illnesses, being female in a male dominated profession and raising five rambunctious children whilst being the wife of the most alpha of males. Mummy T, as we affectionately called her, constantly encouraged me with, "You have got to know yourself," whenever I complained about almost anything. I learnt a lot from her, having survived childhood rheumatic fever, then chronic asthma, ischemic heart disease, angina and finally succumbing to kidney and heart failure.

None of this hindered her achievements, from being a Fulbright Scholar, a linguist and an English Professor! Widely published and respected by all, her greatest achievement was the legacy she left. She taught me and the many others who sung her praises, long before and after she left us, that it's not who you are or what you have achieved that truly matters. It is how you make people feel after an encounter with you. This is the true essence of what I would invite you to translate into how you build your business your way!

No dedication would be complete without mentioning my incredible children: Jerome, Joel, Matthew and Barri-Allison, who have put up with and encouraged my outrageously driven work ethic. And by no means least; my wonderful partner in business and life, my dearest husband, Mark. You are a man amongst men.

You allow me to be ALL of me and for that I am truly grateful. I cannot imagine my journey without you.

And in keeping with my philosophy of being unrepentantly you, I give all Glory to God who has kept me alive and well all these 57 years; still full of hope, vision and bursting with excitement for what is yet to come!

CONTENTS

"In my opinion EVERYTHING we do in life is about sales, but ultimately, it's about understanding yourself, other people and having the skills to sell yourself. The **YOU PRINT™** is a fantastic model to use, not only to build your personal brand, but ultimately your relationship skills and confidence. Bernie Davies lives and breathes what she has created; this is a book not to be missed."

~ Alison Edgar MBE

FOREWORD

Growing up, I never really fitted in. I was the fourth of five children, from a very well respected family established on hard graft, determination and fierce vision. Both of my parents were from humble beginnings and were not about to tolerate mediocrity within their household. Hence, they reared a brood of high achievers with the strength and resilience to match. You can imagine being fourth down the pecking order was not a nice place to find myself for a multiplicity of reasons.

From a young age, I developed an 'and me' personality. I had to figure out how to get noticed, get heard and be valued. I quickly discovered the way to do this was to excel. My mother was a University Professor and so academic excellence was a very valuable currency in my world. At just 4 years old, when we had the weekly in-house spelling and multiplication quizzes (yes we had them) I learnt that if I won, I would get the current prize, be praised, noticed AND be the centre of their attention!

Fast forward to early teens; I started to grapple with not being very well liked in school because of my competitive nature. I used to complain to my mother, who would always respond with the same words, "You need to know yourself." She even told me in Latin at times, "Temet Nosce." It took me 37 years, crossing the ocean and changing my country to truly understand that the greatest achievement I could ever have and the most precious gem I will ever find…is myself!

Who are you? And why does that matter? Who are you when all the voices in your head are silenced? When that whisper in your ear at a young age said, "You will not amount to anything…you're just like your…" Or, "Why can't you be like …?" Or, "We are such and such, that is what we are like for generations and there is nothing we can do about it." When all of that is silenced and you are faced with just you; who are you? I believe that the single most important thing anyone can do is to know themselves. By knowing yourself, you are in a position of power in business. You are able to utilise this knowledge to build an incredible personal and business brand, which will set you apart in the marketplace.

I hope this little handbook, with its practical exercises and tools, will help you to find that uniqueness in you and in your business.

Own it, bottle it and sell it!

MY PERSONAL JOURNEY

In 2006, I moved from Bradford to Cardiff in Wales, (some 260 miles for those who do not know) to a city where Welsh was just as familiar as English. I had the responsibility of networking on behalf of my law firm and in particular its Conveyancing Department.

It was on this journey that I discovered one of the first things we need in order to be able to establish a credible personal brand: the ability to laugh at ourselves and not to take ourselves too seriously. In other words, I learnt how to use potentially embarrassing situations to my advantage.

For example: the day I discovered that my staff member's train being stuck in Mountain Ash did not mean we had just had a natural disaster of extreme proportions in Wales, United Kingdom (UK). For the benefit of those not familiar with Wales, Mountain Ash is the name of a town! I laughed along with the rest (who were doubled up with laughter) when I said it out loud and I have not lived it down to date. However, because I did not take offence and owned my naiveté, people accepted me, warts and all. I pronounced the Welsh words incorrectly and laughed too loudly! Those very things endeared people to me in the marketplace. I was different and refreshing, but most importantly I was GENUINELY different. It was not made up and was therefore consistent. It was WHO they would encounter on every occasion. They could depend on meeting the same Bernie each time and it wasn't hard work for me as I was just being myself.

I still use my distinct (and to some, uncultured) accent to my advantage in business, as it distinguishes me from the rest. It is an immediate icebreaker as it begs the question of where I am from. As most people have either been to or would love to go to the Caribbean, it makes for great conversation. On the telephone I also have an 'edge' as my voice is easily recognisable, and so coupled with charm, it can be an effective way around the most ardent gatekeeper.

STARTING A NEW BUSINESS

There is no question that establishing a business is a very expensive and time-consuming venture. We must, therefore, take a very serious approach and be very thorough in our preparation and planning. Yes, we have got to follow the key steps of our business plans, SWOT Analyses and Financials. But what drives all of that? Where are the legs on that body? Where are the WHY and WHAT FOR? Where is the VISION being personified? How do we establish that? It's all in cleverly establishing and marketing the BRAND!

Anyone who has ever thought about starting a business will admit that whilst it might be very exciting, it can also be a very daunting prospect. There are many benefits to gain, but also many pitfalls and opportunities to fail. Let's get the 'boring' but vital bits out of the way first and then let us look at how to personalise your business venture with your You Print™.

Before we start a business, let's consider these 10 things:

1.   You!

Ask yourself, "Am I ready for this?" We are all gifted and talented in our own unique ways and, based on our differing personality traits, some of us are born entrepreneurs and some academics. Some live for the corporate world and others thrive in front of a computer; changing the world from their bedrooms. Which one are you? Let me help you with that. Not everyone is cut out to run a business. Unfortunately, some people make this discovery after years of struggle, frustration and severe financial loss. You need an entrepreneurial and pioneering spirit to make a success of any business in today's economic climate. You need to have a clear vision and purpose for your business that consumes, excites and drives you.

If this is not the case, you may wish to examine whether you are pursuing someone else's dream and not your own, or whether you are focusing on simply making money. It might be a good idea to re-think that approach. If you are not pursuing a venture that, 'if money were no object,' would still excite you then it is probably not the project for you. If you cannot think of at least three good reasons why your prospective clients would be better off using you, don't for one minute think that they will. If your mind is not whirring with ideas as to how you will make the marketplace discover how great an asset your offering is, maybe you should think twice. If you do not truly believe that your offering compares more than favourably and has distinct advantages from that of your competitors...definitely think again!

And most importantly...if you hate hard work, rejection, budgets, compliance, customer care and sleepless nights then you are in for a shock, as that is exactly what running a business is all about.

2.   Market Conditions

Every day is not a good day to go to the beach! You might have an amazing business idea, marketing and business plan but the timing might very well be wrong.

A simple investigation into market conditions, the competition and the potential gaps in the market for your idea is a must do. It is always best to engage in feasibility studies and take expert advice on whether the market will respond favourably to your offering at any given time. Of course, there are no guarantees, but careful research and planning will reduce the risk of ill-timed ventures.

3.   Business Name

Choosing the correct business name is just as important as being immensely qualified to start your business enterprise of choice. Whilst your business name more often than not needs to indicate what you do, some businesses have benefited from 'catchy' names, which work well with their innovative public relations and marketing strategies.

It would also help if your business name and strap lines used were selected with Search Engine Optimisation in mind. Google is King and the web and social networking platforms are the currency of the day. Research into the best industry-specific keywords provides some insightful indicators to assist in the choice of a business name. I must underscore here that it must be a true reflection not only of what you do, but also WHO you are. Some names that have made me chuckle for example, are 'The Codfather' for a fish shop, 'Sew What?' for a seamstress and 'Wok and Roll' for a Japanese takeaway!

4.   Branding

Branding is everything! It establishes and promotes the identity and ethos of your business and, by extension, its culture. Your business brand tells us the type of service we should expect from you and either establishes or negates (if done poorly) your credibility. Therefore when considering branding, you need to consider the HOW, WHEN, WHY and WHERE of standing out by positively distinguishing your business in an authentic way. Your brand has to be established on your core values, which are then translated into the service delivery, how you train your staff and how you represent yourself in the marketplace. Your brand has to be genuine and authentic. Your brand must be consistent. The brand colours, logo, font type and strap lines must not only be an authentic reflection of your business model but also the message, core values and personalities of the key business partners. Only then will the brand be believable and sustainable.

In addition, the logo created for you must be able to flow seamlessly with all the advertising and marketing platforms you plan to use. For example, if you are planning to network or exhibit at shows as well as advertise in glossy magazines and on all social media platforms, you have to consider whether the design will fit just as nicely on brochures, exhibition stands and business cards as it does on the website and business stationery. I would suggest you take expert branding advice, as your business is worth it.

5.   Message

It's all about conversation in business today. Social networking (both on and offline), more than anything else, has proven that building relationships through conversation is the most effective way to circumvent cold calling and the 'numbers game'. So, what message should your business be sending by way of conversation? It is vital that you identify and establish the key business messages around which your business brand is built. It is even more vital to anticipate the difficulties that might arise in getting the message across to the desired market. Also formulate a clever strategy and implementation plan to overcome all or any of these difficulties.

It is important to understand, however, that whatever the unique key messages your business might send, the most important message a prospective client, joint venture or referral partner needs to hear is what benefits are there for THEM in continuing the conversation with you. If you fail to establish BENEFIT, you will fail to truly engage them and will struggle to win their business.

6.   Website

Your website is your high street shop window. However, it is not meant to be a 'hyped up' fact sheet about your business. Your website should work while you sleep. It should 'dress', 'sell' and 'engage' like you do when you go networking. It should be your business culture personified, or if you are an entrepreneur…it's all YOU! The brand design must be identical to all the other ways you represent your business. The language of the website must in 7 seconds (as that is how long an average 'surfer' stays on a web page) convince the reader that there is a benefit to keep reading and MUST have a call to action. This can simply be encouragement to click for more details, to request a free gift, or to enquire for a quote.

The language of the website must be simple, easy to read and free from typographical errors. The copy must be written using industry specific keywords that Google 'likes' in order to increase your chances of being found on the web. What you offer must be clear. Your contact details and clever means of increasing your database should be considered. For example, an enquiry form and/or a mailing list sign up form can be very helpful. A Frequently Asked Questions (FAQ) page on your website is also a good way of including industry specific keywords on your website. Links to relevant legislation and guidance will also be useful in making your website attractive to Google. It is usually best to seek expert SEO and website development advice and support for this.

7. The Competition

Industry intelligence is of the utmost importance when embarking on a business. I mentioned the importance of a SWOT analysis earlier, where we identify strengths, weaknesses, opportunities and threats at some stage of our business planning process. However, not many of us take this process seriously and truly look at the process as a means of getting a real edge on the competition. Before starting a new business, it would be wise to get to the 'under-belly' of your rivals. Find out where they have their edge, what their clients think of them, what their plans are etc. This is best achieved by strategic networking.

8. Support/Mentoring

We all need support. An extra eye to provide a new or different perspective, unbiased ears to bounce ideas off and an accountability partner are vital to any new start-up. There are many organisations set up to offer this support. Some can be accessed free of charge and others charge reasonable fees. I am a firm believer in the value of mentors and coaches. I believe we should be prepared to invest in ourselves. Why should anyone else invest in us, if we are not prepared to?

9.   Networking

Nothing beats face to face networking in building trust between businesses through relationships. However, you need to be ready for networking, so first ensure that points 1-8 are properly in place. You will then be confident talking with other businesses as you will:

- Look good (after having established a brilliant brand)

- Sound good (after having established your key messages and true benefit to the marketplace, including your edge over your competition)

- Feel good (as you will be confident that you will be able to maintain your first impressions)

All of this is because your business image has been created upon authenticity and supported by expert mentors or coaches.

The most important advice about networking is that it is not a product sales opportunity. Networking is a means of introducing you and your business to the marketplace, to consistently remind the marketplace that you are still around and open for business and to encourage people to want to build a relationship with you and your business. It is an opportunity to sell YOURSELF! Networking skills do not come naturally, especially as we have been told from the playground that we should not talk to strangers! I will delve a bit more into networking further into this guide.

10.   Funding

The greatest hindrance to creativity and productivity is money worries. It is very important to identify funding to sustain your business for at least 6 months. Some businesses are able to borrow the required amount, but more often than not individuals have to wade through the grant system to access any available funds possible. This can be a very frustrating process. Take the time to research and identify any government funded support agencies who are able to make the process that much simpler or seek the help of a reputable business support company. Of course, the best route is to use cash of your own. My best advice is that you should delay launching your business until you have secured the required funding.

INSIGHTS/REFLECTIONS

_____
_____
_____
_____
_____
_____
_____
_____
_____
_____
_____
_____
_____
_____
_____
_____
_____
_____
_____
_____
_____
_____
_____
_____
_____
_____

"Embrace your uniqueness! It is in our differences we establish the distinctions that make us shine, along with all the others brave enough to unrepentantly say, "This is me!""

~ Bernie Davies

BUILDING YOUR BRAND THROUGH RELATIONSHIPS

I firmly believe that we wear 'masks' when we enter the work arena. The main reason for this is that we are not comfortable with who we are. Also, by extension, we do not believe people will be comfortable with us either. We suffer from what we call Imposter Syndrome. Every day we worry that we will get caught out! People are going to find out we are not really who we are pretending to be and 'soon it will end in tears,' are some of the thoughts we struggle with.

I would like to encourage you to believe in WHO you intrinsically are and what you are currently achieving. You might consider yourself to be a fraud because you are painfully aware of your inner turmoil. The many times you have to speak to yourself before attempting that daunting project, hosting that power-packed meeting, or even daring to ring that prospect. But you did it, didn't you? You found the courage to 'fake it' as you see it.

I do not see it that way. I see it as finding the strength to overcome those self-deprecating thoughts and doing it anyway! I see it as winning in life! It is easy to square your shoulders and spout platitudes when everyone around you is cheering you on. However, when the dog just died or you lost your best client over an unfortunate misunderstanding or you've just jumped off the scales one stone heavier - you are NOT a fraud in that meeting with a smile slapped on, pitching like a boss! You are a modern-day hero! The world needs more people like you!

Understanding that truth about yourself is the first step towards being ready to own **BRAND YOU** or what I call your **YOU PRINT™**. It is NOT about:

- Hypocrisy

- Faking it/giving false impressions

- Making false promises and then not delivering

A winning **YOU PRINT™** - the imprint we leave behind whether by default or on purpose – is about successfully balancing the 'face' of our business identity with the 'face' of our persona (personality). With it comes its own unique, attractive and endearing qualities that gain prospects and win business. Each 'face' must be genuine, credible, authentic and attractive. Each persona must operate simultaneously and intelligently within your chosen marketplace. If we use these 'faces' effectively we will win and retain loyal referral partners and clients.

So how do we do that, you might ask? I daresay it is as simple as taking all of you to work. It is not leaving behind the personality that endears us to our friends and families. When we don our work suits and work personas, jump into our wonderfully polished (or if you are like me, much disheveled and abused) cars and hurtle out into the rollercoaster world we call big business, we need to take our personality too. Think about the last person you met where you thought, "Wow, what a lovely person! I would really enjoy speaking with them again." Then ask yourself, "What was it about them that made me feel that way?" I can guarantee that their great job title or their six-figure income were not the reason. Perhaps it was one or more of the following reasons:

- Their sense of humour

- They made you feel special

- They were interesting

- They listened attentively to what you had to say

- They seemed like somebody from whom you could either learn or gain value

I cannot emphasise enough how extremely important it is to be interesting, as well as interested in others, in the marketplace. Professionalism and integrity are paramount, but if we forget that we are humans who require that genuine and subtle personal engagement, our successes will be nominal or nonexistent.

How did I stumble upon this life and career changing 'secret'? My short answer is from my move to Wales from Bradford, via the Caribbean, after a career in Law. As I explained earlier on, everything was new to me in my role as Head of Property at NewLaw Solicitors. I was new to Wales, NewLaw Solicitors was only four years old (practically a fetus in law practice years) and the Conveyancing department that I managed was just six months old! I was faced with the task of pulling together an indomitable team, introducing the firm to the South Wales marketplace and most importantly, stopping the incessant, "New-who?" whenever I introduced myself and the firm!

Within six months of embarking upon what I now

realise was an ingenious strategy (if I do say so myself), I was invited to speak at the National Conveyancing Congress in Birmingham, England. Not as an astute lawyer, as was my first thought upon receiving the invitation, but to explain to delegates how a person should artfully promote, market and collaborate to grow their Conveyancing departments.

The day had come for my national recognition among my peers, but it was not for what I would have ever imagined! You have got to laugh haven't you? So here lies another message. On our journey doing our 'thing', people are watching and picking up on MORE than we can imagine! We do not need to worry about where the opportunities will come from for our business. We just have to focus on doing our business our way with excellence and passion! The rest will fall into place.

And so it did for me. The infamous Home Information Pack (HIP) was launched in 2007. The HIP was a set of documents about a property that had to be provided before a property in England and Wales could be put on the open market for sale with vacant possession. The then-called Red Dragon Radio did not call any of the 100-year-old firms for an opinion. They called Bernie from NewLaw Solicitors, formerly known as 'New-who'! The funny part of the story is that some people actually couldn't stop themselves from asking me - to my face - "Why did they ask you to comment?" Very strange!

The proverbial penny dropped again when our regional Chamber of Commerce was established in January 2009 and I received an invitation to sit on the Cardiff

Council of the Chamber when others had to apply. Me, a virtual 'newbie' in Wales! Within a couple of years I had managed to have more doors open to me at the highest levels and I was connecting more people than having people make connections for me.

The icing on the cake was the run up to Great Britain's 2010 elections. I received telephone calls from Red Dragon Radio and BBC TV Wales to be among the 'leading businesses' within Wales to pose direct questions to the then Prime Minister, Gordon Brown and a select team of incumbent politicians respectively. By then, I had already become a regular contributor (and continue to be) on BBC TV Wales.

In the new business I launched in 2009, I was also delivering training to large and small corporates on how to build their business through branding and confidence, up to and including the Cardiff Council Economic Development Team. I was a speaker at networking business shows and at the Cardiff City Council's prestigious annual business conference, Capital Cardiff, held at the City Hall (delivering 3 sessions in 1 day as I was so sought after). All this happened within four years of living in Wales and in less than 18 months of launching my new business!

My business launch party was full to the rafters with the best of Cardiff and I was in a position to be able to have two of the most prestigious speakers in the region. David Russ, then Managing Director of our regional Chamber of Commerce, and Councillor Neil McEvoy, then Deputy Leader of the Cardiff Council (now a Welsh Assembly member). The clincher was that then Councillor McEvoy was a last minute stand-in for my original speaker, who pulled out at the last minute due to illness. Of course, there are no prizes for guessing the nature of my core business: networking training! My business also encompassed public relations, branding and strategic business development. Since then I have established and run an award-winning restaurant chain, Jamaican Jill's. I also own the Swansea and West Wales franchise of one of the largest networking organisations in the United Kingdom: Introbiz (boasting connections with Sir Alan Sugar, Sir Richard Branson and global motivational icon Les Brown to name a few)! I have not given all of this background information to pat myself on the back or shout my own accolades from the rooftops, but to merely explain to you why I believe so strongly in the principles and strategies that are discussed in this handbook. These are the strategies I discovered that worked for me and they can work for you too, if you apply them.

INSIGHTS/REFLECTIONS

How do people know you? What makes you stand out?

_____

_____

_____

_____

_____

_____

_____

_____

_____

_____

_____

_____

_____

_____

_____

_____

_____

_____

_____

_____

_____

_____

_____

_____

_____

THE ATTENTION ECONOMY
AND YOU!

With business becoming a lot more relational, we have to adjust our business development strategies accordingly. We are hurtling headlong into an ever-increasing 'attention' economy. You only have to take a look at your phone to see that 'noise' is everywhere! I have taken to muting media in my settings as I risk a multiplicity of sounds frightening the life out of me when scrolling and I am sure I am not the only one. So how do we get noticed in and amongst all of this clamour?

 The businesses that will successfully outstrip their competitors are the ones who take the key elements of WHO they are along with WHAT they do and cleverly weave that into their marketing and social media strategy. It is all about the **You Print™.**

"The **You Print™** of the people we send networking becomes the imprint our companies leave behind."

~ Bernie Davies

YOUR **YOU PRINT™**

So, remember what I said about your **You Print™**? Well, we all leave one of those behind when we venture into the marketplace, or simply by interacting with businesses throughout our working lives. Just as we have a unique fingerprint and footprint, we should aim to leave a **You Print™** that positively sets us apart. 'Brand' and 'branding' are pretty commonplace words and are understood, if not applied, by most. I am by no means pretending to be the founder of some new idea. I am saying this old idea has been overlooked for too long!

It has been many years now since Tom Peters, in his book Brand You said, "We tend to erroneously treat our personal image (or brand) and our company image as being mutually exclusive - big mistake!" Tom quotes Martha Stewart as saying, "About two years ago I realised that I was no longer a person, but a brand." This statement is true about all business people - whether we acknowledge it or not. The frightening truth is that we all have a brand; be it by design or default. The age-old saying that, "People tell us who they are," is not limited to our 60-second slot at a networking meeting or a well-rehearsed presentation. It is just as true in the non-verbal messages we send with our gait, demeanor, eye contact and of course that bit of 'je ne sais quoi' that grabs attention.

You might say, "It's easy for you to stand out in your marketplace, Bernie. There aren't many female, Caribbean entrepreneurs in Wales!" Yes, that is true, but I challenge anyone to win the argument that there is nothing unique, different or even what some may call 'weird' about them. In fact, the 'weirder' you might be, the greater the edge and opportunity to stand out and use that idiosyncrasy to your advantage. No one can be as good at being you as you! So, find the uniqueness in you and your business; own it, bottle it and sell it. See how that impacts your year-end bottom line!

Some people have grasped this concept with great success. As examples, Kim Kardashian created an outstanding brand for the voluptuous woman, the unforgettable Michael Jackson and of course, Lady Gaga! I would hope by the examples given, that I am by no means promoting smoke and shadows. Rather excellence, consistency of skill, application and professionalism magnified by inspirational creativity!

Another powerful discovery nowadays, is the value of owning and telling your story. We as a generation have had so much thrown at us and survived so many challenges, that we can smell the 'bull' a mile away! We are hungry for truth and authenticity. We crave learning from real people who have overcome real challenges. These are the people that sell out conferences and workshops. These true modern-day heroes attain through their transparency and vulnerability the status of attraction marketers. People chase them now. They are not only magnates, but they are also MAGNETS.

So, what is your story? What relevant bits of your journey can you use to attract and inspire? How does your personal story impact how you run your business and how much of it can you incorporate into your brand story? Remember it is YOUR business YOUR WAY!

As a Founder or CEO of a large business, you should also consider whether your personal You Print™ matches or conflicts with your company brand or culture. If you agree that a company's culture naturally mimics the leadership style and behaviors of the leader and the senior management team, and if the theory that we lead primarily from our core personality traits is correct, it is therefore reasonable to conclude that the predominant behaviors in a company unwittingly create a recognisable and much more believable company image, brand and 'personality'.

We therefore have to be careful that the behaviours and culture we encourage daily do not clash with or have a negative impact on our carefully created company brand. We are introduced to a business by several means, including the Internet, advertisements and networking. We are served up an 'official brand' on the Internet and in the newspapers and magazines. However, you may agree that the most convincing and effective brand or image of a company is the one portrayed by the people representing it. This responsibility of representation is not limited to networkers, business development managers or even the heads of businesses. Unfortunately, for some businesses, the impact is just as effective in the hands of a telephone receptionist, security guard and the ever-efficient executive assistant.

Undeniably, we individually have a responsibility to

carry out our business endeavors within the marketplace with an awareness of self, our image and personal brand and how it impacts our company brand. It is very important in this ever-increasing jostle to be noticed so that we stand out for something admirable, professional and credible. In essence, we need to realise that the You Print™ of the people we send to network becomes the imprint our companies leave behind. Therefore, we need to use our best endeavours to equip them to leave a great imprint on our behalf!

Exercise 1 (Group)
Practical Steps Towards Your You Print™

Get together with a group of four to eight key, trusted business colleagues. I suggest that this exercise is repeated over a period of time and with separate sets of colleagues for best results. There is space at the end of this chapter to record your answers.

Discuss the following:

- The best qualities in each other, including personal and business skills

- One or more interesting facts in your background that people would not be able to guess

- Is anyone currently in a line of business that they never dreamed they would have been involved in and why?

- Does anyone want a career change and why?

- What is the apparent unique selling point of each others' business?

This exercise should assist in answering the following questions:

- Am I perceived in the way I would like to be?

- Are my personal image and company brand compatible?

- Am I being true to who I really am within the marketplace?

- Am I making a valuable impact?

The other benefit of this exercise is:

- Key discoveries will be made about you and your colleagues, which may increase your awareness of previously untapped value.

- A greater understanding of backgrounds and experiences leads to more meaningful engagement, inuring to stronger bonds of trust. Trust is the key motivator for giving and referring business.

- You may discover your personal and business **You Prints™** and a better understanding of how to purposefully and strategically imprint them upon the marketplace.

EXERCISE 1

INSIGHTS/REFLECTIONS

"The greatest discovery you could ever make is YOURSELF. Not as others see you, but as who you truly are."

~ Bernie Davies!

YOUR **YOU PRINT™** AND YOUR BUSINESS

So you have the desire to build a business or to rebrand your business. How does the **YOU PRINT™** practically apply in this process? The practical **You Print™** exercise is a start. There are other key questions you need to ask yourself to assist you in establishing your unique personal brand. Have a go! This exercise is most effective BEFORE launching a new business.

Exercise 2 (Individual)
Discovering your inner drivers

There are no right or wrong answers. Do not overthink and you can be brief but you must be honest.

1.   List 3 people who inspire you:

    a.   One from your childhood

_____

    b.   One in business

_____

    c.   One personal / friend

_____

2.   List what about them inspires you:

_____

_____

_____

_____

_____

_____

_____

_____

_____

_____

_____

_____

_____

_____

_____

a. Do you see anything in them that is similar to you? (This could be their story etc.)

_____

_____

_____

_____

_____

_____

_____

_____

_____

_____

_____

_____

_____

_____

You might wonder what do questions 1 and 2 have to do with establishing a unique business brand. Well, think about it. Don't we all somehow mimic, or at least try to mimic, those we admire? Sometimes the childhood 'idols' so to speak are reflected in our behaviours. However, if we come to terms with our own core values and identify the influencers, we can take ownership of our developed characteristics and purposely leave those imprints behind in the form of our personal or business brand.

3.   What do you think people think of you? This should be no more than a paragraph.

_____

_____

_____

_____

_____

_____

_____

_____

_____

_____

4.   What has been your biggest 'win' to date? How did that affect you?

_____

_____

_____

_____

_____
_____
_____
_____
_____
_____
_____
_____
_____

5.   What has been your greatest loss? How did that affect you?

_____
_____
_____
_____
_____
_____
_____
_____
_____

Question 5 is very important to grapple with and come to terms with if we are going to be comfortable with who we are. There is this saying, "Success is failure turned inside out." I will go further and say, "Until you've experienced gut wrenching failure at least once in your life and have clawed your way back out of it to the other side, you're a 'has been' waiting to happen."

One of the things you can most certainly be sure of is LOSS. If you've not practiced dealing with LOSS, your 'success' is built on shaky ground and will most likely be short lived. I personally cannot be inspired by a millionaire who doesn't have any story of loss suffered at some point in his or her journey.

6.   If you had to identify the constant 'voices' in your head or recurring thoughts, what would they be?

_____

_____

_____

_____

_____

_____

_____

_____

7.   What would you like people to think of you?

_____

_____

_____

_____

_____

_____

_____

a.   Why?

_____

_____

_____

_____

_____

_____

_____

_____

b.   Do you feel you have ever controlled that?
i   If yes, how?

_____

_____

_____

_____

_____

_____

ii   If no, why not?

_____

_____

_____

_____

_____

_____

Questions 3-7 will help us to better grasp the concepts explored later on in this guide on building confidence and making it your personal gift to yourself. At the end of the day, we have to take responsibility for our personal growth.

8.   Why did you choose your career, business or service?

For this task, record a video of YOURSELF telling YOURSELF what discoveries you have made from your answers that can positively influence how you package yourself and your service delivery.

EXERCISE 2

INSIGHTS/REFLECTIONS

"One important key to success is self-confidence. An important key to self-confidence is preparation."

~ Arthur Ashe

YOUR CONFIDENCE AND YOU!

After careful assessment of the drivers that move us and shape our behaviours, we might come up with one key factor that hinders or slows down our progress. This key factor is often confidence, or a lack thereof. Confidence is best bolstered by a true understanding of ourselves, the reasons we struggle with self-limiting thoughts, how to manage those negative narratives and how to overcome it.

I often use the analogy of building a house to describe how we can effectively build our confidence. I have no reason for this as I am no builder, but I hope you can follow me with this.

1. Laying the Foundations

This is pretty much akin to, and incorporates the journey of, establishing your You Print™. You cannot avoid self-examination, so I recommend the following:

Start managing your mind

This can be very tricky as programming starts early and develops over many years. We might find that we have been programmed to think negatively about ourselves by the people we have known and trusted all of our lives. Changing that way of thinking is NOT a betrayal of those loved ones. It is a well-deserved gift to yourself, for which there should be no apology!

Think about your strengths

- What is it that you do naturally that only other people seem to think is actually a big deal? To you, this gift is just something you do and you have never placed any real value on it.

- What is it you are truly proud of that you can do very well? Celebrate it. Find a way to shout about it (in a nice way of course).

Think about what's important to you and where you want to go

Now this can be difficult as most times we are very quick to list all of the things that matter to our husbands, wives, children and work mates. That will not lead to a better outlook on yourself if you do not also value the same things. If you do not share those values, do NOT use or incorporate them into your business.

Look at the things you've already achieved

- List them and tell them to yourself in the mirror every day until you truly believe in YOU

Commit yourself to success

- Invest in yourself

- Get coaching and mentoring

2. Bricks and Mortar

These are the key ingredients needed to build that confident brand which is uniquely YOU. These are established out of not only your understanding of the vision you have for your business and what it will do for others, but also having a clear WHY for your business. This is how you ascertain what moves and motivates you in your business. The WHY usually dictates the HOW of your service delivery and is the motivating factor that keeps you true to your core values.

Build on the knowledge you need to succeed

- Oprah Winfrey is quoted as saying, "Success is when Preparation meets Opportunity." Always keep upskilling and learning.

Focus on the basics

- Our strategies do not have to be based on expensive or over the top methods. Simple customer service, which builds loyalty, is key. Saying, "Thank you" and showing appreciation goes a long way in business and creates an incredible personal or business brand for you.

- When common everyday acts of kindness lead to a great reputation and feedback, it makes us more confident in the marketplace.

Set small goals and achieve them

- The journey of a thousand miles, they say, starts with one step. Let us not overcomplicate things. Set bite-sized goals, write them down and tick them off. You will be surprised at the confidence boost.

Keep managing your mind

- No one is going to do it for us. I firmly believe that there is a battle for our minds daily that starts first thing in the morning. Whoever wins that battle takes the spoils. I am certainly not giving what is mine to anyone else and neither should you. Not to those dissenting voices in our heads – no way! We have a business to run and customers to serve. We have a legacy to create and teams to inspire!

- So how do we win this battle? We have got to decide that each day is a fresh start. And you are allowed to stop at ANY time, in any day and make that choice. It is just easier to do it first thing, before everything else comes crowding in. So, like I said…you STOP. You might have to shout out loud to yourself to make yourself listen!

- It is a fact that you cannot think a negative thought and speak a positive or uplifting statement at the same time. So here's the strategy: we are going to drown those negative thoughts with positive words. I suggest you grab an inspirational book. My first morning book is the Bible and I go to the verses that tell me how amazing I am and all of God's promises for my life. Yours might be a self-help book or a motivational piece. Whatever your go to for inspiration, please GO TO IT FIRST THING!

3. The Roof

The key factors that keep us 'covered' with confidence and upholds the 'structure' listed above are as follows:

Other people

- Get some tried and tested old friends involved in your journey. Remember the old saying, "There is safety in numbers"? There is also STRENGTH in numbers. It is good to be at peace in our own company and to be comfortable with solitude. However, self-isolation is unhealthy, crippling and diminishes us.

- Get accountability partners who will help you to stop self-sabotaging.

- Get referees who will give you good reviews and pass on great contacts.

Positive Speaking

- If you manage your mind, positive words will follow.

- A positive mental attitude will naturally lead to positive speech.

Appearance

- Slap a smile on your face.

- Watch your body language by keeping your shoulders square, chin straight ahead, arms relaxed and eyes friendly and welcoming.

What factors build your confidence? What could you improve on?

_____

_____

_____

_____

_____

_____

_____

_____

_____

_____

_____

_____

_____

_____

_____

_____

_____

_____

_____

_____

_____

_____

_____

_____

_____

_____

INSIGHTS/REFLECTIONS

"A successful person is one who can lay a firm foundation with the bricks that others throw at him or her."

~ David Brinkley

CONFIDENCE AND SELF CONTROL

What do you allow to creep in? Are you someone who lives life by knee jerk reactions? That is certainly no way to manage your life and by extension your business. We must approach our lives and how we deliver our business services from a position of controlled power. We need to come from a place of quiet confidence which allows us to strategise as well as respond to unplanned events, leading our teams to do the same. How can we inspire and evoke confidence in our teams or customers if we are distracted by thoughts of yesterday's failures, something horrible someone said or overwhelming self- doubt?

If those are the thoughts you allow in and meditate on, you will find that you operate your business in a haphazard fashion, dictated by the way the 'wind is blowing' on any given day.

Practicing the habit of capturing every negative thought that tries to jump the queue when you wake up in the morning, or when you are mid-flow in a business pitch, will eventually empower you to be centred in your business and the delivery of your services. I always believe that everything is about perspective. Whatever you might be going through at any given time, there is always something to be thankful for. It's about looking up and out at the beautiful sunset instead of down at the litter on the streets. It's about appreciating honest feedback and being grateful the customer did NOT tell their friends about that issue but told you instead and thereby allowed you to fix it. It is about being grateful for the redundancy that forced you to harness your creativity and establish an international brand; Lawyer Keri Andriana was made redundant in 2017 and is now the CEO and Founder of Amschela Luxury Handbags (based in Bristol, United Kingdom).

I am aware I have focused on YOU and your confidence a lot. However, your business will not surpass your own limitations. YOU are your most important product.

So now we have built our 'house' of confidence, please bear in mind to protect it from 'invaders'.

- Re-affirm confident thinking

- How do you do that? By literally training your brain and monitoring the thoughts you let in and meditate on. This is as simple as subscribing to positive podcasts or keeping a healthy stack of books which uplift and enlighten. Have you ever noticed how a song plays over and over in your head, or snippets of a movie keep replaying? That is what I mean. So now you realise that by default you have been programming your thought patterns, simply purposefully set about to reprogramme them with positivity.

- List your reasons to be confident

- Remember this is not about being big-headed. It is about a healthy appreciation of all the ways in which you have done well or overcame a challenge or gave someone a hand. We often overlook the good deeds we do as being par for the course. It is not about gloating, but it is about realising we are good people and thereby reaffirming our confidence in and appreciation of who we are.

- Talk to yourself

- Yes, as I have said before, our words matter. Listen to yourself. Catch yourself in the act so to speak! When you hear yourself saying self-deprecating things: STOP! Take that negative statement back and replace it with a positive. You might not feel it at the time but in the same way we can talk ourselves sad, we can talk ourselves happy.

- Practice makes perfect

- Keep at it. The old saying, "Rome was not built in a day" springs to mind. They also say it takes 21 days to form a new habit. What do you have to lose? You have spent more than 21 days doing things that promise no self-improvement so why not give this a shot?

- Avoid self-comparison

- This is the silent dream killer! We are always tempted to look at others and wish we were like them. I once heard a story of a group of people sitting around a table. Each of them felt they were hard done by and that no one else was struggling like they were. They were all wishing they were like one or the other of those sat with them. They were asked whether they would like to trade places with anyone there. They all said yes. They were then asked BEFORE they traded lives, would they like to hear the hardships each one was facing at the time? They all said yes. "Of course, it cannot be as bad as mine," they all thought.

- After listening to everybody and hearing each struggle, they were asked, "Are you ready to trade now and with whom?" Well it should come as no surprise that they all politely declined, embraced their own challenges and left happily thinking, "My goodness, I could never handle all that!" I am sure you get it. The grass might be greener on the other side, but what is buried under it?

INSIGHTS/REFLECTIONS

Record any limiting beliefs/self-sabotaging actions here!

_____

_____

_____

_____

_____

_____

_____

_____

_____

_____

_____

_____

_____

_____

_____

_____

_____

_____

_____

_____

_____

_____

_____

BERNIE DAVIES

YOUR BUSINESS BUILDING/ BRANDING TOOLKIT

Every aspect of life and industry not only has rules, but also needs aids or tools to assist us to achieve expert results. Branding is no different. The tools that I will mention are not exhaustive, but more indicative and instructive. It is my view that each has its own value and the level of results will be in direct proportion to the extent and skillfulness of how we apply them.

After considering and establishing our business idea and the brand that best fits our personal brand, we have to translate this into practical, visible and seamless ways. The following places are where your brand appears for all to see:

- **Website.** Consider colour scheme, content and imagery appropriate to the agreed brand. Build your website YOUR WAY. I most certainly did. Have a look at www.berniedavies.com. My colours, my message, my whole website screams BERNIE! When you go onto my website you not only know what I do, you know what my values are and pretty much can guess what style any training or coaching session will be like with me. This is what I mean by bringing yourself into your business.

- **Business cards.** The same principle applies. Just get an experienced graphic designer and please ensure they reflect your brand.

- **Brochures.** These can be replicated from your

website design.

- **Personal appearance and countenance.** We are
  our brand. If we wish to stand out, we should be
  prepared to make an effort. Think it through. The
  colours you chose for your website should have
  been colours that you like, therefore it shouldn't
  be too difficult to incorporate them in your
  dress/styling. Thankfully hair colours of all types
  are pretty much accepted and celebrated. You
  could therefore stick to wearing neutral colours, if
  that is your thing, and put a splash of your brand
  colours in your hair, or goatee if you're a man.
  These are just some ideas. However, after a
  session or two with you, any skilled brand
  specialist should be able to guide you. I support
  my clients in this way with great success.

- **Nothing beats a smile for an outfit!** You could
  be wearing the best couture ensemble ever;
  without a smile it falls flat. Practice a happy face.
  It is the most winning personal brand ever! Of
  course, it must come from deep within so you
  must first work on a positive attitude, as I keep
  saying, and then a welcoming aura will naturally
  exude from you.

These tools all form a part of the seamless process of
personal and company branding discussed earlier. It
goes without saying that the key message on your
website would be the same ones in your marketing
material and most importantly, on the lips of your staff
members both in and outside of the office. This
message would be the same one agreed upon in the
boardrooms, discussed in departmental meetings and

eventually inculcated in the staff morale, resulting in an amazing company culture - or as some would call it - company personality! Can you think of a company where most people behave the same? Whether it's a good or bad culture, we tend to remember the companies upon whom we can depend for a particular kind of experience, don't we? The aim should be to create positive cultures.

"That might not be as easy as you think, Bernie," you might say. But I would have to disagree. Have you ever noticed how easily we see people getting labeled with '*always*' or '*never*' doing one thing or another? Usually the ones spreading this narrative feel very passionate about whatever it is they are complaining about. As they are focused on the few times this offending thing happened, they completely ignore the times it DID NOT happen.

By the same token, I am positive we can immediately think of at least one famous celebrity singer who cannot truly hold a tune, but whose charisma, beauty or sex appeal overshadows that completely. The wise amongst us manipulate this knowledge of the human tendency to positively affect reputation. It is simple: do one or two very outstanding things often and consistently enough, and others will believe that you **always** do this amazing act and **never** do anything else wrong! The secret is getting enough people in your business to consistently perpetuate your vision and ethos and the marketplace will inevitably 'buy-in' to your brand. This will eventually become self-perpetuating.

INSIGHTS/REFLECTIONS

"I firmly believe that there is a battle for our minds daily, that starts first thing in the morning. Whoever wins that battle takes the spoils."

~ Bernie Davies

PERSONALITY PROFILING AND YOUR BUSINESS

As important as it is to understand and establish your personal and business brand, it is equally important to be aware of others within the marketplace. If we believe that establishing our YOU PRINT™ is a vital approach to adopt, then understanding the 'face' or persona of our business associates and potential clients is crucial.

Personality/Behavioural Profiling is important in respect of building winning teams, dealing with conflict resolution in the workplace and developing winning negotiation skills. In this section, we will look at how understanding personalities within the marketplace will positively impact your business growth. I use behavioural profiling through personality testing to help my clients understand who THEY are in the marketplace, but more importantly, it helps them to recognise who OTHERS are when networking. It gives them an advantage when selling or negotiating.

The method I use categorises personalities into colours. I will give a brief outline and overview, as it is important to your business success to understand these principles. The personality types are: RED, YELLOW, BLUE and GREEN.

Here are the characteristics of the personality types. For ease of recognition they have been somewhat exaggerated; please do not take offence.

The Yellows

- They love to help people

- They will do more for others than themselves

- They are the kindest and most pleasant people

- They are professional huggers

- They make great leaders

- They have integrity

- They are always talking

- They never listen! They're not being rude; their minds are going at such a speed that they don't have time to listen

- They will never follow up with people; they are too busy meeting new people

- They are big picture people

- They are action people

- They are team players

- They love meeting new people; to them there's no such thing as a stranger

The Blues

- They are professional

- They are the accountants, the solicitors, the engineers, bookkeepers, scientists and deep thinkers

- They are analytical

- They require lots of information

- They are happy to engage in meaningful conversation

- They will respond to you with lengthy emails

- They will expect you to approach them in a professional manner

- They will require more than one meeting to decide

- They could be 'snobbish,' and so you need to establish your expertise to get their attention

- Name dropping does not work with them

- They are keen to know how respected YOU are in YOUR field of work

- They are impressed if you thoroughly researched them before a meeting and make them aware of how much you know about them and what they do

- They require lots of proof

- They won't be pushed

The Reds

- They like to be in charge/to be the boss

- They like to tell people what to do

- They are great organisers

- They are all about the money

- They don't listen as they already have the right answers

- Every red you meet thinks that they are yellow

- They love competition

- They love recognition

- They will make the most money in network marketing

- They will do things their way

The Greens

- They are process driven

- People consider them to be boring but that is far from true

- They care about your feelings

- They do not like to offend

- They take a lot of time to make decisions

- They want to be right

- They are not huggers

- They are great leaders

- They know all the information

- They will be with you for a long time

I can hear you asking me to justify you going through

this long list about colours. The truth is it is difficult in this short guide to unpack the science behind personality profiling. This brief section has been included for understanding, because any source which attempts to explore business principles and relationships needs to pay homage to personality profiling. Admittedly, it can be difficult to determine someone's personality colour and I am certainly not going to pretend I can teach you about it in this short business guide. You may go to my website htttp://www.berniedavies.com and book a meeting with me or a personality testing session to get a deeper understanding of behavioural profiling. Behavioural/Personality testing is also done with teams in order to support healthy workplace relationships and effective team management.

When we go networking, we are not able to look at someone and immediately get an idea of his or her personality type. That is why conversation and taking time to listen and know people is so important. Especially in the networking arena, it is good to regularly attend the same groups and become a member in order to develop ongoing relationships. I always recommend the 80/20 rule when first meeting someone; I try to let them talk 80% of the time. Here are some questions you can lead with when you meet someone in the networking arena:

1.   "What do you do for a living?"

2.   "What do you do in your spare time?"

3.   "What do you like most about your job?"

We definitely need to be asking more open-ended or leading questions with a view to unlocking this kind of useful information much earlier than we currently do. For example, questions like:

- "So have you always been in banking?"
  You might find out he used to be a car dealer, like my previous bank manager. This will probably tell you this person might not be as reserved or risk averse as their current job might suggest.

- "You know, I have always wanted to run a recruitment agency. Is practicing law what you always wanted to do?"
  You may find out that she was in marketing and public relations for many years before becoming a Lawyer! I know someone like that. This Solicitor was therefore very open to new and exciting projects and did not need every exchange to be conservative and ultra-professional.

- "So, tell me a bit about yourself, the person behind your business."

- The possibilities are endless with this type of icebreaker and you are sure to unearth some interesting information upon which you can build a valuable connection and maybe even referral partnerships. I will take this opportunity to point out that not every prospect is a potential customer. This is why we need time to get to know as much as we can initially about the new people in the marketplace. By engaging them in conversation you are likely to identify who is a client, who is a client later on, who is a referral partner and who is a perfect person to collaborate with on projects.

These types of questions will no doubt provide you with good clues as to personality colours, but they are not foolproof. Sometimes a person's job does not match their personality; they could still be finding their 'true North,' so to speak, or they might have, through a promotion or an enforced job change, been placed in a position which is by no means indicative of who they are.

Just try your best, as you're not always going to get it right, but you will be spot on sometimes. Sometimes the best question is the open one, "Tell me about yourself and what you do." This leaves you open to getting a lot of information. Listen. Read between the lines. Listen to what they have mentioned and more importantly, listen to what they have left out! Sometimes, the clues to understanding an individual are the obvious or expected information they did NOT give you. Clever listening is key! Only then will you develop those key connections and collaborations to win in your business!

Let us unpack this a bit more and examine how our insight into a prospect's personality colour would instruct how we invite them to events, for example. You might want to ask yourself, "What would make that person want to attend or sign up?"

Here are some tips when inviting people to a meeting or presentation based on their colour. It should also instruct us as to which events are best to invite them:

Yellow you would emphasise the opportunity:

- To help care and nurture other people

- To have fun and meet new people

- To talk a lot

It would be best to invite them to hospitality events where you have lots of key contacts to meet them. They would be very blessed by you if you are well connected. Name-dropping works for them, so 'drop' to your heart's content!

Red you would emphasise the opportunity:

- To make lots of money

- Of being in charge

- To organise people

- To get plenty of recognition

- To showcase themselves

The reds are best invited to a money-making opportunity or a networking event where they will be seated at the head table with celebrities or millionaires. They would need to hear how much money you made from previous meetings and how your connections resulted in positioning you in high places. Of course, please remember, we are always being credible and honest. So please do not exaggerate and make false promises.

Greens you would:

- Give them lots of information

- Show them your business presentation over the Internet, since they don't like meeting people

Inviting a green you would say something like, "I am attending a meeting and I need your opinion. Nobody will try to sell to you. We do not have to participate. We can just sit in the back and you take notes and let me have your feedback afterwards."

The greens are therefore best suited to meetings where there is a speaker and there is no obligation for them to present who they are to the room. They will not be happy if they are pounced upon during the meeting to give feedback before everyone.

Blues you would also:

- Give them lots of information

- Show them your business presentation over the Internet since they don't like meeting people

Dependent on the type of business you are in, and the leverage you have, you would do well inviting a blue to speak at an event you are hosting, or to be an expert panelist. A blue would also be very keen to sponsor an event where they would be given an opportunity to give a brief presentation showcasing their knowledge and expertise.

Other types of events that a blue would be happy to attend are those where lots of decision makers and those influencing policies and laws are involved. Whilst they might be thorough and appreciate a lot of paperwork, they might also be great orators and comfortable with talking to large groups as opposed to multiple individual conversations. Again, I must emphasise this is not foolproof and you will be wise to be guided by your intuition and take things slowly before deciding the best methods of approach.

Personality/Behavioural Profiling and YOU!

The wise and recommended response to this information would be introspection with a view to identify which 'colour(s)' we are. My view is that in reality we tend to be a combination of personality types. We can also operate stronger in one personality type than another, based on the context we find ourselves in. A client once told me that I was an 'orange', a combination of yellow and red, and I found that to be intriguing and accurate.

"So, what does that have to do with brand and business building, Bernie?" you might ask. "Everything!" is my answer. If the key to business growth is to make effective connections, strike up mutual interest and eventually develop relationships which result in financial benefit, then it's not exactly rocket science to figure out that it would be vital to be able to communicate and interact with individuals in the ways that they feel comfortable. Anyone who ignores this basic truth does so at their own peril.

For example, if you attempt to greet someone with a hug and they extend a hand, therein lays the clue. Do not attempt to hug them next time around! Also, if you are having a great discussion with someone with whom you would like to collaborate on a venture with and they say, in response to a suggestion, "Great, send me an email and we can discuss it further," therein lays another clue! This person has strong 'blue' traits. They do not want to be rushed into a decision without a lot of information and time to consider it carefully.

You might be a 'red' and can already see what, in your eyes, would be a significant mutual financial gain. Despite having great difficulty grasping what they could possibly have to think about, resist the urge to telephone the next day asking, "When can we start?" Always remember to consider the question, "What's the thing that motivates that group of people?" Remember, you are not your prospects, but you can think like them.

Hopefully the message is not lost. The key is to allow individuals to open up and reveal some of WHO they are and not just WHAT they do. The true value is that in unearthing these key facts, you are able to identify whether there is anything in their current or past involvements that provides an opportunity for you to either deal directly with them, or get referred to someone in their sphere of influence.

INSIGHTS/REFLECTIONS

NETWORKING

It is impossible to talk about building your business and your brand without mentioning networking. The networking arena is the most common place where businesses establish their brands and attempt to win business through building relationships. So I guess it comes as no surprise that I own and operate a networking franchise as well. I am extremely passionate about building your brand and your business, and equally passionate about ensuring you network effectively to get that brand promoted effectively. When we go networking, we should have both a long-term and a short-term strategy.

- Long-Term Networking Objectives:

- Journey to the bank - earn money

- Gain new business

- Increase income

- Increase profitability

- Achieve sustainability

Why is that the long-term goal? Why is it not top of the short-term list? Isn't it really all about winning business and making money? Not at all! That might be the end game, but the primary objective when you network is to sell YOURSELF, NOT your business! You want to wow your networking colleagues with your personal brand. You want to showcase your core values by how you respect them, listen to them and ask if you can be of help. Remember their name and develop rapport. You cannot underestimate or circumvent the 'know, like and trust' process!

Simply put, the short-term and main networking objective should be to get people to want to see and speak to you again. Other equally important short-term networking objectives are:

- To pique interest

- Enhance reputation

- Raise company awareness

- Maintain old contacts

You should not 'crank up' the sales process until you have networked and followed-up effectively and you are in a meeting with the prospect.

INSIGHTS/REFLECTIONS

YOUR VISION/VISIBILITY

Credibility and visibility are to business, what love is to marriage ... although some of you might disagree!

We have unpacked what makes for a credible business strategy in the earlier chapters by looking at how we marry WHO you are to the WHAT, HOW, WHERE, WHY and WHEN of a business. I would like to delve a bit deeper. I am going to set a picture and hopefully we can unpack a few more things together. Let us consider the following practical scenario:

A business has been in operation for just over 8 months. The directors are meeting to review the last 8 months' performance. They will also create a budget, produce a marketing, sales and business plan for the next 12 months and agree on all other pertinent factors to the growth of their business. The accountant has given a review of the projections collected from all the departments, the marketing and sales results are reviewed and strategies are formulated. Within that plan, certain key target markets are agreed.

Some businesses make the mistake of not going that step further by looking for key non-competing businesses with whom a referral partnership can be developed. There should also be attempts at identifying from among these non-competing businesses, reputable prospects with whom a joint venture would help to raise their profile and establish credible visibility. Any good strategist would examine their marketplace and use referral-building techniques to break into the difficult target markets.

On the other hand, wouldn't it also be absolutely foolhardy if this hypothetical business failed to pass on their strategy to the team that networks on their behalf?

Wouldn't it also be unfortunate if the team that is public facing, has no clear grasp of the business' brand and message? Even more so, can you contemplate that after all that effort they 'dropped the ball' because they were not taught how to communicate and engage effectively with the varying personality types they might encounter?

This is why ongoing training of staff and coaching of key individuals within our teams is vital. This is also why Behavioural Profiling is beneficial, as it helps managers understand how to communicate with individual members of their teams appropriately to win their support. Managers are thereby empowered to take that one step further to becoming inspirational leaders!

Whilst it is important to pursue new business and connections, the most important market to network and develop is the one we already have! Client retention is one of the key methods of growing any business. Our existing client base is undoubtedly our most important target market. They are our best marketing tools with free word-of-mouth advertising at our full disposal. Sometimes we are so keen to win new clients that we overlook this goldmine. We do not focus on customer relations as we are always angling for the next referral.

Here are a couple of ways in which you can serve your

existing clients:

WOW Them!

If at this stage of the book you are not able to think of a few ways to distinguish your business and service delivery, I have not done a good job. There are many ways clever business owners have managed to wow, woo and keep their clients. One method is the strategic use of the Customer Relations Management system (CRM).

Any company that does not adopt some form of client profiling is missing out on a very valuable tool. This helps staff relate to a client, based on their individual preferences. Imagine how valuable it would be if staff were trained to use personality profiles to instruct the way in which each client is communicated with and/or approached. I think it would be absolutely amazing if the CRM systems were coded accordingly! There is no doubt that miscommunication leading to offended clients and complaints would be significantly reduced. It would also positively affect how requests for renewals or repeat business were handled and received.

Be Dependable!

I cannot emphasize enough the importance of authenticity in our business building strategies. Dependability (crucial for client procurement and retention) will not be achieved without authenticity, as it's very difficult to be consistent in any lie. Some may even successfully argue that it takes one particular set of skills to win business and a completely separate set to keep it. However, I would like to suggest that both skills are best optimised when applied simultaneously. If the required method to win business is innovation and panache, you cannot then offer a service that has no heart, is non-communicative, distant and disengaged. We have to remain constant in our message. This is crucial and must also be instructive when we are recruiting staff to service our clients.

One obvious recurring theme in this book is that all staff play an important role in the success of our business. And, let us not forget as I said earlier, that the You Print™ of the people we send into the marketplace, becomes the imprint our companies leave behind.

How can you WOW your clients?

_____

_____

_____

_____

_____

_____

_____

_____

_____

_____

_____

_____

_____

_____
_____
_____
_____
_____
_____
_____
_____
_____
_____
_____

Why do your clients depend on you?

_____
_____
_____
_____
_____
_____
_____
_____
_____
_____
_____
_____
_____
_____

INSIGHTS/REFLECTIONS

_____

_____

_____

_____

_____

_____

_____

_____

_____

_____

_____

_____

_____

_____

_____

_____

_____

_____

_____

_____

_____

_____

_____

_____

_____

VISIBILITY TIPS & STRATEGIES

The best way to stay visible in a credible way is to have others shouting about you. Yes, you have to have your social media and marketing strategies cleverly mapped out, but these are only part of the plan and not nearly as effective as others spreading the word about you or you being seen in the right places and with the right people.

One strategy is getting to know key networking event organisers and offering to help them with the events, sometimes by simply greeting, signing people in or introducing speakers. You will immediately add a level of credibility to your image in the eyes of other attendees. People will naturally assume you are a person of influence and worth knowing.

Here are some other ways you can get referrals, build credibility and enhance visibility!

1. ASK!

It is simple. If you do not ask and do so quickly, it will not happen! I always suggest that on social media, we GIVE recommendations first as that usually prompts people to respond with one for you. It is a lot easier to get them motivated in this way, than a text or phone call requesting a review. Of course, you need to be sure they are happy with your services first as a bad or lack lustre review is not beneficial. If someone is happy with your service and excitedly tells you about it, ask them for the review immediately. Do not lose the moment. If they are busy people, why not write the review and send it to them for approval?

2. Do something ordinary in an EXTRA-ordinary way

What do I mean by that? Well everyone is 'parading' themselves online at the moment. We are all jostling for that same space, for the same audience and for the same thing…getting noticed!

However, it seems like much of the same most of the time. It becomes monotonous. For example, we all have become 'gurus', posting inspirational quotes all over social media. I am just as guilty and it has its place.

The ones who will cause us to stop mid-scroll and pay attention are the ones who are either doing something extra-ordinary or look interesting. You may have the most incredible content to share but, make no mistake, no one will listen if it does not have an edge. This kind of edge almost always comes from a unique personal, innovative and creative slant, which is either never-before or rarely seen.

You know I am right. Think of the last thing that stopped you mid-scroll on social media, or the last speaker you heard which you cannot get out of your head. Get your thinking caps on guys! Let us dig deep into ourselves and come up with unique and show stopping ways we can get seen!

If you are struggling with this, get help. Find an expert who will help you to pull to the forefront all that you have inside, package it as uniquely you and then serve it up HOT!

3.   Build a referral funnel

Create a referral form. One easy method of getting referrals is offering a commission, although not everyone is motivated by money; there are still a lot of people who are happy to refer you if you have taken the time to WOW them as I mentioned earlier. However, it is always good to reward them in some way as they have put their name on the line by referring you.

The best reward you can give is ensuring the referred customer gets the best service ever! Try to strike the balance between novel and gimmicky when coming up with ideas. It takes time and effort, but it's worthwhile getting a great set of incentives together.

Some methods of incentivising referral partners are:

- If you are a consultant, offering a free session is an idea

- Discounts on your service

- Rewards – these should not exceed 15% of revenue earned from the referral

- Invite them to events and provide full hospitality

- Sponsor an event of theirs

- Donate to their charity

Think of how you can put an interesting spin on these basic methods.

Here is another idea: why not set up a podcast? There are so many free apps online. Invite your referral partners and key contacts with a non-competing business to be showcased on your podcast. Place this podcast on social media. They will be grateful. They will share it with their audience and you will get noticed in a good way.

You can do the same with video interviews using Stream yard or Zoom. Getting these positive interviews on all social media platforms immediately exposes you to your guests' network and widens your audience. It also enhances your credibility.

Our current clients, as I said earlier, are our best advertising tools. Keep building relationships with them. Continue to find out if there are ways you can help them. They will be your best supporters and will no doubt tell others about you. Also, do not be afraid to ask them if they know anyone else that needs your support.

This question is best posed just after the sale, or when you have completed a great job for them and they are exuding satisfaction. That moment is golden. Ask for referrals then. Write them down and act fast.

4.   Use your website as a referral tool

For example, you can add buttons such as:

- Click here to earn rewards
- Invite your colleagues

- Forward to a colleague

Of course, it is not a one size fits all approach when it comes to these strategies. Remember it is 'Your Business, Your Way'. Your business and your website might not suit this method, but you can find clever tools to capture the data of visitors to your website and follow up with them in an ingenious way. One less used referral and visibility tool on your website is hosting the interviews with other experts or podcasts you create with other non-competing experts. This will drive traffic from their followers to your website and showcase YOU and what you do.

Website testimonials

Detailed testimonials about your service delivery are very useful and are great advertising. I suggest we constantly update our websites with our testimonials. Photos and videos are a great touch.

Remember the 'givers gain' concept and offer to put a testimonial with photo etc. on someone else's website. If they are amenable to it, you could add your logo and a link through to your website and vice versa. Video testimonials for others are a great visibility strategy and please use testimonials everywhere such as your website, brochures, social media and voicemails.

5.   Track referrals

- Know what works. Nowadays useful marketing tools exist to track performance of most online marketing strategies. Get in touch with an innovative and switched on marketing team, as they will be able to use links to track performance on your websites. Facebook also has pixels you can add to your website that allow you to not only track performance but also to capture data for subsequent follow up and loyalty building.

- Target top performing customers and referrers and keep finding ways to keep them happy. Find out what makes them tick and give them more of the same.

- Remember 'givers gain' and be a referrer yourself. Never be seen as someone who takes with nothing ever going out from your end to your business community. It is sometimes as simple as:

- Sharing other business colleagues' posts on social media

- Liking and commenting when your colleague gets a good review online

- Sharing on social media how much you enjoyed an event hosted by a colleague or a book someone wrote or a talk they gave

Finally, I would like to encourage you that, in the pursuit of establishing your vision in a credible way and building a visible brand of which you can be proud, you have to be committed to consistency. There is no quick fix and all the strategies need to work seamlessly and simultaneously. There are some constants, which you need to employ to remain 'top of mind' in the marketplace.

Nothing will take the place of daily phone calls or

emails to follow up on 'warm' leads. We need to spend at least one hour each week researching social media and other key sectors for leads. We should be aiming to add at least three new contacts per day to our CRM system and should invite someone to an event once a week. As I said earlier, catch up with old clients (I suggest at least five per week) and let them know you are available.

Help build your credibility and visibility with philanthropy. Volunteer and engage in charitable causes.

Show up at a high visibility event at least once a week or as often as possible. I used to be accused of being up for going to the opening of an envelope - I will take that! Have lunch or a coffee with an influencer, a referrer or collaborator at least once a week. In other words, keep busy, be consistent and be strategic. I must underscore that all these activities must be carried out with integrity, honesty, authenticity and a good dose of personality!

INSIGHTS/REFLECTIONS

CONCLUSION

Well, there you have it! That's how I started and how I continue to develop and build my networks throughout the United Kingdom and beyond. I have purposely steered clear of outlining social media platforms and their place in your business branding strategy, except to say that branding must be seamless and consistent across ALL platforms.

My aim at this stage of your journey is to simplify and impart the art of personal interaction and its never-ending and increasing value to grow your business in this ever-increasing attention economy. To ignore its value is to stunt your business growth.

Business time moves in light years today. We cannot miss a beat; we have got to pursue our business vision and establish credible visibility, by staying true to WHO we are and WHAT we want to achieve through this knowledge in our businesses.

As for me; I am the things that move me, anger me and excite me. I am that which I yearn to do, if only so those that matter would be proud and happy for me to get on with it. I am that memory I hold on to, that is the safe place I run to when all the world is crashing down around me. I am the pursuit I would follow every day of my life if money were no object. I am that thing that I do so easily and expertly, that I take for granted and never for one moment think, "I could turn this into a multi-million-pound earner."

I am who I am and NOT what I do. I am not what

others think of me…I am what I would dare to dream I could be, if only I could silence that dissenting voice in my head. I am the fierce passion that ignites within me, when I'm faced with certain people, places or things. Why do those things affect me and not others? These are the clues to who we are, why we are here and what we should be doing about it. These sentiments and more will hopefully help you to build YOUR BUSINESS YOUR WAY!

NEXT STEPS

As you can tell from the way this guide has been presented, it invites a response. I am hoping to evoke thought and I am bringing a call to action. There are so many points where I hope you stopped and considered; in particular, the questionnaire that I do hope you filled out. I purposely included some pages for you to write notes as I am hoping this book becomes a companion and a constant reference point. I strategically made it small enough for your handbags, man bags or laptop cases. I would like you to use this book to start conversations with your colleagues. It would also be great to delve more deeply with you into all or any of the areas discussed on a one to one basis or with your teams. There is so much more to explore.

So many of us are at differing stages of the business building process. I do hope my suggestions about factors to consider have added some value, such as your YOU PRINT™, confidence building, harnessing your power, understanding your marketplace, valuing your customers and most particularly: the importance of consistently striving for excellence.

You have invested your money in this book and your time to read it. There are lots of action points which you need to address before you forget and slump into mediocrity and anonymity. There is extra notes space at the end of this book and remember - I am here to help and you also have people in your circle who can. In any event, if this book demonstrated that you need help in any way, do NOT hesitate to reach out and get that help!

BERNIE DAVIES

ABOUT BERNIE

Author, Speaker and Business Strategist, Bernie Davies
has trained hundreds of businesses from the Private
and Public Sector, as far back as 2009. She has trained
in-house for Cardiff Council Economic Development
Team, Johnson & Johnson, Welsh Language Board,
Chwarae Teg Agile Nation Project and 4Ward
Development to name a few. Bernie has
singlehandedly delivered countless monthly sell-out
training seminars to multiple hundreds of businesses in
South Wales. She regularly sits on awards judging
panels as a Business Specialist. Bernie has been, and
continues to be, a regular BBC Radio Wales
contributor and media personality.

Bernie continues to build a career as an entrepreneur,
business strategist, motivational speaker and author,
now launching her second book. In 2010 Bernie
published her first book, called 'TwoFaced
Networking', which has helped hundreds of businesses
learn how to become effective at networking. A serial
entrepreneur, in 2012, she launched and operated for 7
years a much-loved chain of restaurants called
Jamaican Jill's. Bernie owns Introbiz Swansea and West
Wales, a successful networking franchise of Introbiz
UK and is the CEO & Founder of Bernie Davies
Global Ltd.

She has served as a Dynamo Role Model for the Welsh
Government, was among the founding council
members of the South Wales Chamber of Commerce,
Chair of the Neath Chamber of Trade and sat on the

Neath Town Centre Consortium. She has received numerous accolades including 2011 Finalist Best Female Newcomer and Outstanding Contribution by a Business Woman in the field of Charity in Welsh Women Mean Business Awards, voted Top 100 Business Woman in Wales 2017 (IAM WOMAN Awards), Top 100 restaurant in Wales 2018, Best Caribbean Restaurant in Wales 2019, Swansea Black Icon 2019 and Excellence in Business Award 2017, which was awarded at the Sennedd for Black History Month.

Bernie works with entrepreneurs and individuals to master the principles she explores in this book. Further information on what Bernie does can be found at **http://www.berniedavies.com**

You may email enquiries to:
bernie@berniedavies.com

INSIGHTS/REFLECTIONS

"Daily battles are won or lost in the first 5 minutes you open your eyes!"

~ Bernie Davies

Printed in Great Britain
by Amazon